How to Practice Empathy

Connect Deeply with Others and Create Meaningful Relationships

by David Leads

This book is published by Relationship Up. Relationship Up publishes content on the relationships we have with ourselves and the relationships we have with others. Topics to help you be a better you. Check us out on the web!

www.relationshipup.com

Copyright © 2014 Relationship Up. All Rights Reserved. This book or any portion thereof may not be reproduced without the prior written permission of the publisher, except for the use of quotations in a book review. To contact the publisher please visit our website.

Legal Disclaimer

This book is presented to you for informational purposes only and is not a substitution for any professional advice. It is the reader's sole responsibility to seek professional advice before taking any action on their part. The contents herein are based on the views and opinions of the editor and publisher.

While every effort has been made to present accurate and up to date information within this book, the editor and publisher do not assume and hereby disclaim any liability to any party for any loss, damage, or disruption caused by errors or omissions, whether such errors or omissions result from negligence, accident, or any other cause.

The editor and publisher accept no responsibility for any consequential actions taken, whether monetary, legal, or otherwise, by any and all readers of the materials provided.

Table of Contents

Introduction

Chapter 1: What Is Empathy?

Chapter 2: Have More Satisfying Personal Relationships

Chapter 3: Establish Closer Connections with Friends and Family

Chapter 4: Understand What Your Loved Ones Need and How You Can Help

Chapter 5: Manage Conflicts with People In Your Life

Chapter 6: Treat Those You Care about the Way They Want to Be Treated

Chapter 7: Know What to Expect

Chapter 8: Connect with the Larger World

Conclusion

Introduction

Your friends and family members can offer you support and make your life more joyful. When all is well between you and others in these close relationships, your life is not only more pleasant, you also have added strength to face life's many challenges.

Sometimes, though, the connection just doesn't seem to work. You feel alone and distant from the very people who have the potential of making your life better every day. You don't understand the way they feel or what they need from you. And you feel powerless to change the relationships so they benefit both you and the loved ones who surround you.

The good news is that you can take control of your own actions in each situation. You can be the influence that creates a more positive connection in all of your close personal relationships. If you find it hard to fathom what is causing this disconnect, you can learn an important tool to have closer and more fulfilling relationships.

The tool you need most is empathy for each person in your closest circle. When you practice empathy for others, you tend to bring out the best in yourself. Why?

It is because you are more focused on others and the greater good instead of being self-absorbed. Additionally, you inspire others to follow suit and treat you with respect and loyalty.

So, how do you achieve this amazing connection? You learn how to empathize with others and communicate that empathy to each of them. The focus of this book is to explain the benefits of empathy and provide you with tips and exercises to help you learn to practice empathy in your everyday life. The first step is to understand empathy more fully and accurately. Once you understand that, you can move on to developing the empathy you need to improve relationships with the people who are most important in your life.

Chapter 1: What Is Empathy?

Empathy can be a difficult concept to grasp. The word has gained a lot of attention in recent years, but it is rarely defined in a way that is easy for most people to understand. On top of that, the term is often confused with other similar terms. Here is a basic definition of "empathy" followed by a list of those closely-related words and how they differ from it.

Empathy Defined

<u>Empathy Is an Emotional Understanding of the Feelings of Another</u>

One way researchers look at empathy is as "affective empathy." These are the responses you feel when you take on someone else's emotions long enough to understand the situation. You do not lose your own perspective, but you do connect with them on an emotional level that recognizes what they are going through and how they feel. You do not judge them or try to fix the problem. Instead, you place yourself in their perspective and validate their emotions.

Empathy takes place in the present moment. There is no reference to past events or feelings. You are with the other person in that moment and feeling what they are going through. To affectively empathize with someone else, you imagine yourself in their situation or imagine how the other person might feel. Or, you might empathize on a deeper level if you have been through the experience. You mirror back the other person's emotional response.

Empathy Is a Cognitive Function

In addition to the emotional response you can have, empathy can also be defined as a type of thinking. You reason out how the other person feels in the situation by seeing things through their perspective. This is called "cognitive empathy."

Comparisons between Empathy and Similar Words

Empathy vs. Sympathy

When you feel sympathy, you notice how the other person feels and give them advice or comfort. Most often, when you are feeling sympathy for someone, you bring up your own experiences and compare them to those of the person who is suffering. You have not been in their situation, either physically or through your imagination as with empathy, yet you recognize the feelings they are having and try to make them go away. You can offer them comfort and allow them to feel connected and not alone.

Empathy vs. Compassion

While empathy is about relating to the other's emotions, compassion is more about your own feelings of concern for the person. You might worry about the other person and think about ways to improve their situation. You want to help them, reduce their suffering and increase their quality of life. You show your compassion by your actions rather than your words. Although the two terms are different, empathy is also the first step to helping someone in compassionate ways.

Empathy vs. Pity

When you are truly empathizing with another person, you put yourself on their level and understand the feelings they have from that perspective. Empathy brings people together through mutual understanding and appropriate support. Pity separates people. When you pity someone, you see them as a charity case and consider yourself in some way better than they are. Pity can be destructive to the other person's self image because they feel you are looking down on them. And, indeed you are. Pity rarely if ever helps anyone.

Now that you know what empathy is and what it is not, you can begin to see how having empathy can improve your life and the lives of those around you. You can increase the empathy you feel toward others, and you can practice empathy in all your relationships.

Chapter 2: Have More Satisfying Personal Relationships

When you have satisfying relationships with those close to you, your life becomes more joyful. You not only feel happier in the good times, but you also feel love and support when times are hard. You can have closer and more positive relationships with your close friends and family members by practicing empathy in everyday life. First, here is an explanation of what it means to have a satisfying relationship.

What Are the Hallmarks of a Satisfying Relationship?

Empathy – You cannot have a healthy, satisfying relationship if you do not allow yourself to be vulnerable enough to see things from the other's perspective. You have to make an effort to understand their emotions if you want a strong and positive connection.

Rapport – You need to feel comfortable being around and sharing time with your loved one. You may feel this instantly, or you may need to work on it by experiencing and communicating empathy.

<u>Respect</u> – Respecting someone else is a way of valuing their thoughts, opinions, decisions and emotions. You appreciate them for who they are now. Empathy can help you feel that respect in a very real way.

<u>Trust</u> – When you trust someone, you know they will treat you the way you want to be treated. You believe that they will act responsibly in the relationship. When you show empathy for another person, you enhance their trust in your loyalty and commitment to the relationship.

<u>Interdependence</u> – In an interdependent relationship, each person has something valuable to contribute. By the same token, each person can accept the benefits of being in the relationship. You do things for each other without thinking of personal gain. Empathy helps you understand what the other person needs so you can increase the interdependence in a healthy way.

<u>Openness</u> – A satisfying relationship is one in which you can share your personal thoughts and feelings without fear of ridicule or judgment. When you practice empathy, you encourage the other person to be more open with you in the future. In fact, the act of being empathetic is based in an openness of heart and mind.

Mutual Expectations – In a healthy and satisfying relationship, the two of you are on the same page about what to expect. For example, if a man expects that a relationship will be a long-lasting and close one, but the woman only wants to have a casual and temporary relationship, they do not share mutual expectations of the relationship. You need to find out the other person's intentions through empathizing with their feelings and recognizing their perspective.

How to Have Relationships that Enrich Your Life

Healthy relationships are well worth developing, but what do you do if your relationship is weak or dysfunctional? Those kinds of relationships do nothing to make your life better, and in fact may make it worse. You can use empathy to improve your interpersonal relationships. Here are some of the ways to do it.

Understand and Appreciate What Others Have to Offer

Do you feel that your relationships are one-sided and that you do all the giving while the others just take from you? If so, perhaps you do not appreciate what the other person brings to the relationship. Take a moment to sort it out.

Write down the name of a person you are in what you consider a one-sided relationship with. Below it, write the person's positive qualities. Do this as a brainstorming exercise where you write anything that comes to mind without judging it. Next, go through all your answers and circle the qualities the other person has to offer that can enhance the relationship. This exercise can help you realize why you want to be in a relationship with them and why you value them.

Now, put yourself in the other person's perspective. Which of their qualities or attributes would they want you to acknowledge? When you are with your close friend or family member, show them that you appreciate these things about them and value them as a part of the relationship the two of you share. One way to do this is to ask for help with something they excel in – be it an emotional, physical or creative task. It might be surprising to think about, but asking for help can actually improve a relationship, especially if you have taken on the role as the strong one in the relationship previously.

Focus on the Positive without Denying Reality

Look for the good in your friends and family members. Focus on what is positive about the relationship. Think about what each person brings into your life and how they impact the world for the better. Recognize each person's special gifts, talents and strengths. When you keep these qualities as your main focus, you realize that there is something in the relationship worth holding onto. You value the other person more, because you clearly understand their significance and worth in your life and the lives of others.

Yet, you cannot hide from reality. You still need to acknowledge difficulties in your relationships. That is the only way you can make friendships, romantic partnerships or family relationships stronger and more resilient. When you approach these problems with an empathetic mindset, you can begin to work out the problems in a way that is satisfactory to both of you.

Notice and Deal with Personal Differences

Empathizing with someone does not mean abandoning your own perspective or experiencing their emotions from your own viewpoint. To truly empathize with someone, you need to notice and recognize the differences between the two of you. When you put yourself in someone else's position, consider how you would feel if you had their personal background, experiences and qualities *and* were in their situation. To step into their true perspective, you have to take all of these things into account.

As you observe and interact with the other person in a relationship, you can become more aware of the ways you are different from them. Accepting these differences is crucial if you want to have an open, honest and satisfying relationship. The second step is to appreciate the differences and realize their value.

Finally, respond to the other person in the way you now know they would like instead of treating them the way you would want to be treated. As it turns out, the Golden Rule is not as helpful as it might seem. The best way to deal with personal differences is not to treat others the way you would want to be treated, but to treat them the way you have realized they want to be treated based on your observations, experiences and empathetic imagining.

Listen and Communicate Empathetically

How often have you expressed your thoughts reasonably and thoughtfully, only to be ignored? Most people have had this experience at some time or another. The problem is even worse when you do not know exactly what you want to say, as is often the case. This lack of communication can lead to misunderstandings and even broken relationships. So, what can you do about it?

Focus first on listening to the people in your life. Specifically, practice active listening. The first step is to hear what the other person is saying. Next, you check your understanding of what the person is saying by repeating what they said in your own words and asking them if that is what they meant. If you did not understand, ask them to tell you again and try once more to summarize what they are saying. If you did understand, go on to the next step.

The next step is to listen to anything else your friend or family member has to say. Ask questions to clarify anything you do not understand or to get more details. When you understand their story, think of how you would feel if you were this person dealing with this situation. Use your imagination and reasoning to get in touch with the other person's perspective and understand what they need. You can only communicate empathetically after you have experienced this shift in perspective.

Now, you are ready to communicate your empathy. What can you say to express the experience you have just had? You do not need to share how you practiced empathy; in fact it is better not to. Instead, pay attention to the other person in the present moment. Tell them that you understand why they are feeling the way they are. Let them know you care and are there for them. Do not judge them; accept them for who they are in the moment. Make physical contact if it is appropriate. Offer a hug or hold their hand. Whatever you do, maintain the focus of the other person, how they feel and what they need from you.

Chapter 3: Establish Closer Connections with Friends and Family

If you want to get closer to your friends and family, you are not alone. Life in the 21st century can be fast-paced and can fracture even the closest relationships. You might not see your siblings or parents for months. And if you have grown children, they may have little time for you. Many people do not have a network of friends because they are too focused on their careers. Friends and family often take a back seat to what seem to be more pressing responsibilities and pleasurable pursuits. Yet family members and friends can help you deal with these difficult tasks and enjoy your pastimes more. Just as important, you can help them in the same way.

Benefits of Strengthening Connections

Becoming more connected with your friends and family is not something to do because you are "supposed to." It is something you can do to enrich your life. When you have more satisfying relationships with those you want to be close to, you reap numerous benefits for yourself. You also make those people's lives more fulfilling. It is a win-win situation. What benefits would you like to see when you improve your relationships?

Security

Security is one of the most basic human needs, coming only after survival needs like food, shelter and breathable air. Yes, it is that important. Navigating life on your own, without close personal connections, is a shaky proposition at best. You do not know who to trust. If there is something that you physically cannot do alone, you usually have no one to help you unless you pay them for the assistance.

Close relationships offer you several different types of security. For one, you know there are people who care about you every day, no matter what happens. Then too, you get the security that comes with being connected to people who will back you up in a crisis. You do not have to worry about losing everything, because if you have positive close relationships, your friends and family will do everything in their power to see that you are not hungry or homeless.

More Realistic Self Image

Self-esteem has become an overblown concept. Parents are encouraged to praise their children for completing the most minor tasks. Some adults offer themselves the same type of praise in the hopes that it will make them feel better about themselves.

Having a positive view of yourself is important. You need to feel good about who you are and what you do. But without the honesty of people in your close circle, you can easily get out of balance. Besides that, when you tell yourself you are amazing when you do not really feel you deserve special praise, you feel like a phony.

Close connections with others allow you to see yourself as others see you. You do not have to accept their perceptions as reality. But these glimpses into how you are perceived help you find new ways to improve your life. With a realistic self image, you are more open to emotional growth and maturity. This realistic and positive self-image thus enhances both your life and the lives of those around you.

Improved Physical Health

Negative emotions can cause physical aches, pains and ailments. When you feel all alone with your emotions and hold them inside, you can experience: back pain, heart palpitations, stomach upset, changes in appetite, fatigue, headaches, high blood pressure, ulcers, insomnia, stiff neck, sexual problems, lightheadedness and other physical problems.

Having someone to talk to about your sadness, anger or fear helps you deal with the negative emotions and your physical health can improve dramatically. This is an important reason to develop and maintain healthy connections with people you care about and who care about you.

Improved Mental Health

The same negative emotions that can cause physical problems can also be a part of a bigger mental health issue. Why are you sad, lonely, afraid, bored or angry? The reason may stem from something physical, a specific situation or long-term negative habits of thought.

When you are surrounded by a close group of friends and family members, you can get support for these issues. You can share your thoughts and feelings openly and honestly. Sometimes a family member or friend can help you find a solution to a problem that is causing you emotional pain. Other times, they can empathize with you in a nonjudgmental way when others cannot do the same. And, if you have a serious mental disorder, friends and family members are crucial to your well-being.

Empathizing with others can improve your mental health as much as having them empathize with you. When you practice true empathy, you look at things from a fresh perspective. And, if you are mired in sadness and self-loathing, having connections with others can help you see your own worth and contributions to the world as well as the positives in your life.

Increased Happiness

Some people claim that they are happy on their own and do not need friends and family to get what they want out of life. And there may really be moments when you enjoy spending time alone. Independence is definitely a positive quality to develop. But you also need to balance your independence with strong connections with friends and family members.

When you have people who are close to you in healthy relationships, you can increase your happiness. As you get more connected with your closest circle, you begin to share in their happiness and find opportunities to share yours with others. You see the value others bring to your life. And, while you are doing this, you can help others increase their happiness, too.

How to Get More Connected

Once you realize the value of establishing and maintaining close relationships that are strong and healthy, you can begin the process of connecting with others on a deeper level. Many people who are alone imagine that others make connections automatically and without effort. And it is true that some people tend to make connections more easily than others.

Yet even if you have always found it hard to interact with friends, family members or people in general, you can learn how to do it. The first thing you need to do is to be open to the possibility that you can have a close relationship with the person. Then, you can start practicing methods to create and enhance those relationships.

<u>Practice Active Listening in Daily Life</u>

Active listening is a specific skill you can work on and increase day by day. It is not just a handy tool to bring out under special circumstances. Instead, you can cultivate this habit daily and make it a part of who you are.

Make it a common occurrence to listen closely and non-judgmentally to what others have to express. As you do, people begin to trust you more and start coming to you when they need to talk. You become a significant part of their lives, just as they become important to you.

What is more, sharing your thoughts and emotions comes easier when you have developed this closeness with them. By listening actively every day, you model the behavior you would like to see in others. Often people pick up this skill just by watching you do it. You build your own unique support network, and at the same time, you provide support to those around you.

Check Your Perceptions by Asking Questions

If you have read this far, you already know you can improve your active listening by asking questions. But do not think you need to reserve this skill for deep, personal conversations. Your friends and family will likely appreciate your thoughtfulness in making sure you understand each situation as it happens. You do not have to be annoying with your questioning and do it constantly. But any time you feel confused or unsure of what is unfolding, in each of these moments you can gain insight into what others are expressing.

As you spend time with others, make it a habit to check your perceptions. After all, no two people think exactly alike or feel the same way. You can practice empathy to your greatest ability and still miss something important in what the other person is saying or feeling if you do not ask questions. In fact, asking questions and checking your perceptions actually helps you empathize more effectively.

Realize Differences

When you are trying to reach out to your friends or family, you can easily make false connections based on mistaken ideas. When you do this, the relationship cannot be strong. It is likely to fall apart at the first sign of trouble unless you correct your faulty assumptions.

It is natural to think that everyone you care about sees things the same way you do. Fortunately, every person brings their own ideas and personal qualities into the relationship. This is one of the most helpful parts of being in close relationships; you get to understand problems and deal with difficulties from more than one perspective. When you recognize the differences in other people you are close to, you can fully appreciate who they really are – to you, to themselves and to others.

Try this exercise to get in touch with the differences between you and each member of your close circle:

Write your name on the top left of a paper. Now, write another person's name on the right. Along one side of the paper, write down qualities that you value and admire. Next, make a checkmark beside each quality you believe you have. In the column under the other person's name, make a checkmark for the qualities you see them as having. Now, hold the paper up and look at the checkmarks.

In nearly any relationship, you will see that all the checkmarks do not line up. You are not the same as any other person, and no other person is identical to you. By doing this exercise, you can see what the others bring to your life and what you bring to theirs. You can appreciate both sides of each friendship or family connection and take that understanding into the relationship daily.

Take On Others' Perspectives

You can take on others' perspectives during the course of your daily life. This allows you to become more connected to the people you come in contact with every day. Remember to maintain your own perspective. Avoid getting lost in other people's problems. Know that they are the other person's issues every minute you spend taking on their perspective.

People who are just learning to consciously practice empathy sometimes have the notion that they are not doing it right if they are still in touch with who they are. These mistaken seekers want total immersion in the being of the other. This is neither necessary nor desirable. If you totally took on the position of someone else, you would not be able to offer the help they need in the moment. You would be just as confused, sad and helpless as they are.

Yes, it is a good practice to see life situations from someone else's viewpoint. It is even fine to experience their feelings in the moment. The key to maintaining a healthy balance between yourself and a loved one is to connect in the moment through empathetic perspective-taking.

Then, just as important, you need to recognize and understand your own unique perspective. Honor your friend or family member by sharing in their experience – either by literally stepping into their shoes for awhile or by empathetically imagining their situation. And never forget to honor who you are and the perspective you bring to the relationship.

Communicate Empathy in Everyday Situations

When you first start actively practicing empathy, others are almost always surprised by the changes they see in you. As you become better at it, they begin to realize that you have just become a more valuable member of their close circle. It might take awhile for members of your family or friends to feel safe enough to share their innermost thoughts and feelings with you.

If you want to become closer and more connected, you need to practice communicating your empathy with each member of your close circle in normal, everyday situations. It is this habit that inspires people to trust you and open up to you. As you learn the skills of empathy, your close friends and family members can also learn them indirectly by watching you practice them.

The resulting relationships are stronger, more flexible and more beneficial to both than any other relationships you might have had in the past. Nurture these relationships by practicing the skills of taking on others' perspectives, recognizing differences, checking your perceptions and listening actively in every interaction.

Then, communicate the empathy you understand and feel. It is one thing to see from the other's perspective. But the real value comes in connecting to the other person you choose to have in your life. Let them know you understand. Tell them when they have every reason to feel the way they do. Notice their pain, but do not try to fix it right now. Understanding needs and finding solutions can come later. For now, simply stay in the moment of sharing the connection you and the other person have created.

Chapter 4: Understand What Your Loved Ones Need and How You Can Help

Empathy is not all about making your own life more pleasant and satisfying. It does do that. But also, it offers benefits to the people you care most about in your life. Only you can take charge of your thoughts and behaviors. In many cases, it will be up to you to practice empathy when no one else in your close circle of friends and family are doing it. After all, the fact that you have become interested in practicing empathy does not necessarily mean others have reached the same point in their own journeys.

That being said, your path in life is just as important as anyone else's. If you are ready to practice empathy, then open yourself to the possibility that life is going to change for the better for everyone concerned. And, when you are fully engaged in life, you also bring something valuable to the lives of those around you.

Benefits of Recognizing Your Loved Ones' Needs through Empathy

Practicing empathy holds many benefits for both you and the people you want to be closer to in your daily life. In addition to enhancing those connections mentioned earlier in this book, you can be a positive influence for all your friends and family members. Here are some of the ways you can live a fuller life through understanding their needs and desires.

Create a Positive Environment

Present day families are notorious for bickering, and individuals can be selfish and self-involved. There can be a lot of anger, hostility and hurt feelings within a family, and even close friends can get upset with you and others. The resulting environment can be stressful for everyone in the group. Wouldn't you like to live in a more pleasant and positive social situation? You can do it by using empathy to understand better the needs of your friends and family members.

When you, and eventually others in the group, understand what each of you needs, you can create an ambiance that is peaceful, friendly and even joyous. You can work out disagreements in a gentler way. You can virtually eliminate all that hostility and discord within your group. You all become a team engaged in making each other's lives better rather than a random group of individuals each fighting for their own way. Again, you cannot control what others do. But you can be a role model for practicing empathy to learn the needs of others. And, you can inspire others to do the same.

Care More Deeply about Your Loved Ones

By realizing and communicating about your loved ones' needs, you can develop much closer bonds with them. You find yourself caring more deeply about your close friends and family. But is this really a benefit? After all, it can be painful to understand someone's needs if there is nothing you can do to help.

Yet, caring more about your loved ones can help you be more engaged in their lives. It can also make you a stronger person with a more congruent self image. Here's how: If you think of yourself as a good person (and why should you not?), then acting with compassion and caring for others makes you feel more comfortable in your own skin. You demonstrate every day that you are who you think you are. This makes your life much more fulfilling and satisfying.

Of course, when you care more about the people in your close group of friends and family, you make them feel more loved and respected as well. Ultimately, this can come back to you in the form of better relationships and more people caring about you, too.

Inspire Others to Consider Your Needs As Well

People who are emotionally healthy enjoy having a sense of reciprocity within their relationships. They do not want to come off as the one who is always needy and stressed out. They want to give as well as receive. When they see you making changes and thinking about their needs and the needs of others in your close personal network, they usually want to be a part of the positive change.

Even people who are emotionally strung out or confused can sometimes see the value of thinking of others when they are exposed to it enough. Think of yourself as a leader in bringing about positive changes within your group. And, when things begin to change, the others can often make the leap to trying to understand what you need as well. Whatever you do, it can affect those around you. By practicing empathy to understand the needs of others, you can inspire them to get in touch with their stronger, healthier selves.

Offer Needed Help

When the people closest to you are struggling, it is natural to want to help them. If you have no clue about what kind of help they need, you might feel powerless. You cannot offer them anything of value in the situation. And if you try to help them without understanding their needs correctly, you can create more problems than you solve.

By practicing empathy to learn what can improve your friend's or family member's situation, you know what kind of help to offer. Offering appropriate help not only makes things better for them, but it also creates the positive relationship with them that you seek.

How to Get in Tune with Your Loved Ones' Needs

Once you learn the benefits of understanding the needs of those closest to you, you can accept the challenge of being a better friend to all of them. And the process you need to follow is not mysterious or difficult. All you need to do is to follow a few basic guidelines and you can begin to see their specific needs more accurately.

<u>Listen and Pay Attention to Body Language</u>

As you practice active listening with a distressed family member, you need to realize that the words they say do not always convey what they are really feeling. Pay attention to their voice inflection and gestures to notice feelings the other person might not even be aware of. If your loved one says everything is fine but continually looks down rather than ever making eye contact, chances are they have a problem they need to solve.

Remember that you are not listening to pass judgment or give advice. Instead, watch the other person in the relationship carefully to empathize on a deeper level. For example, you can usually tell immediately if your loved one is overtired simply by noticing how they stand or sit in a chair. Are their eyes clear and open as usual? Or are they fighting the urge to fall asleep? In this case, you could offer to relieve them of some of their workload or watch their children while they get some rest. And in some cases, their body language is the only way you know they have this need.

Notice How Your Loved One Reacts to Problems

Many people try to cover up or bury their emotions concerning problems. But in the moment that the issue arises, you can often get a glimpse into how they truly feel. That unguarded moment when they get unexpected bad news or suddenly realize a loss can be very telling. You may see tears gathering or a flash of anger cross their expression before they hide away their feelings.

Take this opportunity to find out how you can help them. You might say something like "You seem sad about the news. Do you want to talk about it?" When you do, you open the door to a closer relationship and the possibility of helping them find a solution or comfort for their problem.

Avoid Judging

Always remember that when you are practicing empathy, the point is not to judge the other person's feelings, thoughts or actions. Instead, it is to get in touch with who they are and how they feel in this given situation. You can help them have a more realistic view of themselves by being open and honest about your own thoughts and feelings. However, that does not give you license to look down on them for their reactions or need for help.

And, if your loved one always hears judgment and blaming from you, they have no reason to open up to you in the future. If you want to build a long-lasting and close relationship, the way to do it is to be accepting of the other person as they are in the moment.

Concentrate on Ways to Help

Practicing empathy is the quickest and truest way to discovering needs and helping your loved one overcome them. Here is how it works: First, you empathize with someone to understand what they are going through and how they feel about it.

After that, you can focus on helping them find solutions. You can step back into your own perspective and ask what they would like to do about the problem. Find out what their ideal solution would be. Now, you know what they need and the resolution they are seeking. You are in a much better position to help them than you ever were before.

As you stay alert to your friend's or family member's words, voice inflections, gestures and body language, you learn what they need. Go beyond that understanding and get to the point of understanding how you can help. Then, follow through and provide whatever help you can. Do not do it to be thanked or rewarded. Do it out of caring that the other person's needs are met. When you do, your relationship can grow stronger and more positive.

Chapter 5: Manage Conflicts with People In Your Life

Did you know that empathy can be so powerful in your relationships that it can help you avoid or resolve disagreements and misunderstandings? You can settle verbal fights and even prevent physical assault from happening in some cases. When you practice empathy, you can become a peacemaker in your daily life. You can bring your family and friends closer and create function where dysfunction once ruled. And, you yourself can enjoy many different benefits from this valuable tool.

Benefits of Reduced Conflicts

Some families like to argue and fight more than others. In fact, many families share a belief that airing emotions loudly and frequently is the key to better relationships. Actually, there is much evidence to support the idea that this is actually detrimental, not only to families, but to the individuals within the family. It is one thing to express emotions, but constantly emphasizing the negative emotions is not a healthy way to build friendships or family bonds.

On the other hand, some families hold in their emotions so much that they do not form the intimate bonds that are so crucial to family cohesiveness. So what is the solution? Practicing empathy as you relate to each other and resolve differences can provide a middle ground that is peaceful yet honest. Here are a few of the positives you can expect in your relationships when you put empathy theory into practice.

Longer-Lasting Relationships

What can cause a breakup with your significant other, the loss of a friend, or a fractured family? Most often it is the arguments and disagreements between you that cause the split. Misunderstandings may start the decline of the relationship. Petty quarrels may cause the two of you to become more irritated with each other. And eventually, if the arguments become intense enough, one of two things happens. Either you break up or you hold onto a dysfunctional relationship and live in misery. Wouldn't it be better to do things differently than to suffer the loss of a spouse, girlfriend of boyfriend, or a dear friend?

People who practice empathy in managing their conflicts can appreciate each other's viewpoint and find civilized ways to work out their differences. They can experience more profound and meaningful moments with their loved one. They can bring something valuable to the relationship and accept the positive qualities of the other person. And, because of all this, they can have healthy relationships that last for a lifetime.

More Peaceful Relationships

Stress between two people in a relationship can show up in very physical ways. Some romantic partners', friends' or family members' arguments can heat up rapidly and even come to blows. Besides the danger of bodily injury, stress can lead to a variety of medical problems. So, getting rid of the discord in relationships is not only emotionally more functional, but contributes to your physical well-being.

If your relationships are not generally peaceful, imagine what it would be like to get along well with your friends and family members. You could wake up in the morning and enjoy the start of a new day with confidence that you and those you hold dear can work out anything that comes up. You could meet after work for an evening of fun, knowing that the other person will not harm you, either emotionally or physically. And, you could spend your time together building the relationship rather than tearing it down.

Show You Care

When you make the effort to manage disagreements and even physical fights, you show your loved ones how much you care about them. You make a special effort to bring peace and harmony to each relationship. You help them de-stress and enjoy their lives more fully. You can be the one to start the two of you on better path to the future. You have always had the possibility to choose this road. Now, though, the choice is much simpler and more obvious. When you begin to practice empathy in your relationships, you make the way to that higher road faster, easier and surer.

When you show you care, the other person can come to understand your sincere desire to stay in the relationship because you express this caring so well. The way this benefits you is that it gives you the kinds of friendships and family relationships everyone needs to be emotionally strong and healthy. Mutual caring between you and each other person creates a connection that you can feel good about and rely on in happy times, rough times and everyday life.

Using Empathy to Manage Conflicts

As a person who has studied and learned how to use empathy, you bring an important skill to every relationship you are now a part of, as well as relationships you enter into in the future. It might seem like an impossible task right now to manage the discord in a relationship, especially if the two of you are often at odds. But you can accomplish it using empathy, not only for the big fights but for the everyday squabbles, too. Don't try to rush the process. Just follow it as the need arises, taking each moment as it comes.

Consider What the Other Person Feels about the Issue

The first step to practicing empathy to resolve interpersonal problems is to practice the active listening you have already read about. Listen with your mind set on understanding, your eyes focused on their body language, your ears tuned to their voice inflections. In other words, be open to the emotions they are displaying. Ask questions to make sure you understand the situation and the person's reaction to it clearly.

Before you start trying to haggle out your differences, go within yourself and think about what the other person is feeling. What is their perspective? Considering what you know about this person, how are they likely to take the situation? And, what emotions are they expressing to you? Breathe deeply in and out, and just let the answer come to you. When you reach the point of seeing the issue from the other person's viewpoint, start engaging with them again.

Honor Your Own Perspective while Respecting that of Others

As you connect to the other person on both mental and emotional levels, remember to consider your own position in the disagreement. This is an important part of practicing empathy to resolve conflicts. The reason is that if you do not take care of yourself, you cannot expect others to do it. You are the guardian of your own well-being. Unless you honor your own perspective, you put the burden on others to do it for you. So, really, honoring yourself as you work through the issue is being kind to the other person, too.

At the same time, honor the other person's perspective. Don't crawl so deep within your perspective that you forget about the other person's viewpoint. While you are seeing from both perspectives simultaneously, remain alert and aware of what is going on. Carrie J. Menkel-Meadow, an expert in alternative ways to resolve conflicts including legal ones, uses the term "process pluralism." And it is definitely a process rather than a single thought or action. The other person might go through a range of emotions, especially if the issue has been on their mind for a long time or if it is an issue about a trauma in their life. As the emotions change, you can continue to practice empathy to gain perspective, considering both your changing perspectives on the situation. It is a balancing act in every moment. However, if you take it calmly, the process is easy.

Work Cooperatively to Find Solutions

When practicing empathy in managing conflicts, it is important to understand that conflicts are all about change. It might seem like you are having the same old arguments over and over. But what you have to realize is that the fact that you and/or the other person is putting effort into expressing their opinions in this way means that one or both of you want change. If not, the two of you would fall into uneasy silence. You are engaged in a process.

The process might at some point slow down, but you can't assume that it is not continuing to be an issue you need to work on or that it is not changing and evolving over time. As long as you are living, change is occurring in every molecule of your being. So, it is reasonable to assume that relationship will also change. Find the heart of what needs to be changed and you can discover the deeper issue.

For example, a husband and wife might continue to argue over housework that doesn't get done. Each one accuses the other of being a "slacker" and failing to live up to their responsibilities. This may seem like a stagnant issue. In reality, they both want a change. They both want to have a clean house. When they come together to discuss it in an empathetic way, they can work out a solution that creates a change and eliminates the argument. Even more important, they can work out the deeper issues of their relationship such as respect, trust and caring.

Continue the process of resolving the conflict by promoting an atmosphere where the two of you can work together to find answers and make decisions on what to do next. As you are discussing the issue, continue to use active listening, and rely on it more than you do on expressing your own opinions of how to solve the issue. Instead of saying, "This is what we should do," say "What do you think we can do to solve this?"

The question is the key to making headway on a difficult-to-resolve conflict. Do give your ideas, but also put these in the form of a question, such as "What do think it would be like if we did X?" Listen to the other person's answers and pay attention to ideas they bring up during the conversation. Be flexible in your thinking as you add their ideas to your internal list of possible solutions. When you ask enough questions, you can find the point where you both can come to an agreement. That is one of the many powers of empathy.

Chapter 6: Treat Those You Care about the Way They Want to Be Treated

Earlier in this book, there was a mention of the Golden Rule and the fact that it is not a way of treating others with true empathy. This saying is not completely wrong. It is right up to a point, but it does not describe empathy. For that, it just needs a few more words added to the end of it. "Do to others as you would have them do to you" *if you were them and in their position*. And these words also need to be added to the Silver Rule, as in "Do nothing to others that you would not have done to you" *if you were them and in their position*.

Benefits of Acting Empathetically

Perhaps the idea of reciprocity with an included element of empathy was the original intent of what most people in the Western hemisphere now know as the Golden Rule. The first known written record of social reciprocity was in the Code of Hammurabi, an ancient record of laws from Babylon, dated at around 1750 BCE. In an earlier code, the Code of Ur-Nammu from about the 2100 BCE, reciprocity is not mentioned. And, it is likely that the idea originated long before it was written down anywhere. This religious and ethical concept dates back to ancient times in so many different cultures that it is difficult to say.

Maybe it is just in modern times that we have lost the meaning of it. Or, it might be that we are just now arriving at the most helpful interpretation of it for the first time as a culture. History is interesting, but it does not answer every question. One thing is certain: treating others with the same respect and consideration as you would like to receive in their position provides many benefits.

Show Others You Respect Their Individuality

When you truly empathize with another person, you see them as being different from you. They are an individual with their own personal qualities, needs and contributions to the relationship. You realize just how unique and valuable they are as a person. You recognize their strengths and understand what is harder for them.

Yet, this information has little impact if it doesn't change your behavior towards them. Treating others as they want to be treated expresses your appreciation of the differences between who you are and who they are. It shows them that you value them as a person.

Here is an example. Imagine that Paul has always lived in the shadow of his more successful sister, Martha. When Paul becomes upset about work, Martha can practice empathy by putting herself in Paul's position to understand that he feels resentment towards her on this subject. By the same token, when Martha has marital troubles, Paul might empathize with her and see that she feels afraid of having to choose between losing her husband or her career.

In either case, one sees the other as an individual with needs, desires, emotions and personal strengths and weaknesses. And, more importantly, they give recognition to this fact in the way they behave towards each other.

Reduce Frustration for Both of You

Another benefit of treating others as they want to be treated is that you and your loved one can both avoid feeling irritated and frustrated. The fact that you are trying to practice empathy shows that you desire to care for others more deeply and to be a positive influence for those around you. Yet if you only understand and do not act, others will not appreciate your efforts. How can they when there is no evidence of them? This situation can leave you feeling frustrated and annoyed. When you take empathy to the highest level by acting on it, you avoid this uncomfortable feeling.

Also, if you are committed to practicing empathy, you can become frustrated if you treat others as you and not they want to be treated. You think you are doing a good thing for them, and yet they don't respond the way you had hoped they would. You might question whether empathy is really helpful and give up on it. Or, you might feel like you can't make a difference in your loved ones' lives. While you cannot control the reactions of others, you can have better success by treating the other person as they wish to be treated.

You can also help your friends and family members feel less frustrated. The reason is that you can help them feel understood. If you treat them the way you and not they would want to be treated, then they might feel like you don't understand them at all. The best way to make them feel you understand and appreciate them for who they are, is to consider their wishes as you act on your empathetic imaginings.

<u>Inspire Others to Respect You More</u>

By respecting the individuality and wishes of those around you, you change the relationships. Using empathetic action, you can remold the relationship into one where the other person's needs are recognized and acknowledged with appropriate behaviors. This means that, not only do you respect them, but they are also inspired to respect you in the same way. The best way to earn someone else's respect is to respect them in their own position.

Using Empathy to Tailor Your Responses to Others' Needs

Some people seem to empathize with others and treat them they way they would like almost automatically. However, even if you do not have this natural ability, you can still learn to behave in ways that specifically address the needs of loved ones. The key to appropriate actions is to observe, imagine and behave with empathy.

Observe Your Loved One's Reactions

Having an active imagination alone does not guarantee that you can behave empathetically. First, you need to observe your loved one so that you can base your imaginings on something real. Start by paying attention to your loved ones' reactions to offered comfort and assistance. What seems to make them happier, more productive and more stable as a person? What responses seem to make them angry, uncomfortable or dysfunctional?

Pay attention to their reactions whenever someone offers advice, support or aid. Then, as you begin practicing empathy, continue to notice their reactions to your efforts. Your loved one might be surprised when you first start changing the way you respond to them. Eventually they can get used to the new you and you can see how they react to you once they are comfortable with the changes.

Imagine Empathetically

Before you start trying random behaviors to help someone in an empathetic way, you need to use your imagination. The next exercise can help you practice the process of treating others based on empathy for their situation. You won't have to do this every time once you get the hang of it, but it is a helpful way to begin.

First, go somewhere that you can be alone and quiet. Now, think of your loved one's personal qualities. Name them silently to yourself. Next, think of the ways you have seen your loved one react to offered help. Finally, set your imagination to work. Picture a scene in which your loved one displays concern about some need by expressing it through words, body language or actions.

After you have an image or an idea of how the other person feels about the situation, think of what you can do to make them feel better and help them. Use your imagination further to picture how they are likely to react if you follow through with actions you deem appropriate. Once you come to a conclusion about how they would like for you to treat them, you are ready to act.

Behave Empathetically

Now, you can begin to offer comfort and assistance to your friend, romantic partner or family member based on what you know about them and your empathetic imagination. You might feel uncomfortable or unsure of yourself at first. Don't worry. With practice you will get better at helping them meet their emotional and physical needs.

The first time you try to deliberately behave empathetically, just focus on choosing words and actions based on your conclusions. Calm yourself before you engage with the other person. Be kind and gentle as you offer what you believe they need from you.

If at all possible, talk first. This gives you the best option for checking your perceptions and knowing what the other person truly wants from you. But if you have concluded that they need you to take certain actions without talking about it, proceed with caution and check their responses along the way.

Later, after you have practiced behaving empathetically for a while, you can stay in the moment more and be more flexible as changes happen. And remember that behaving empathetically is usually a process rather than a single action.

If you do feel frightened or unsure of yourself as you make those first tries, don't let your insecurity hold you back. Choose a situation about which you are as certain as you can be of your loved one's response. Have faith in yourself and in the other person that your efforts will produce something positive. Then, go ahead and do what you know is best.

Even if your plan does not unfold the way you hope it does, there is still value in the attempt. You can analyze the situation after the fact to learn more about practicing empathy with that person. In the larger scheme of things, your first try is only a fraction of the good you can do for yourself and others. Step out boldly and act empathetically as soon as possible. Assure yourself that only good can come when you are open, honest, caring and empathetic. Then, make that first attempt at treating others the way they want to be treated.

Chapter 7: Know What to Expect

Have you ever tried to be there for a loved one and then walked away feeling that your efforts were not appreciated? Or that you must have said the wrong thing? If so, it likely happened because you didn't know what to expect when you started the conversation. Although you can't predict every reaction or always say the right thing, empathy does put you on more solid ground in the interaction. Instead of randomly trying this and that to soothe and pacify your loved one, you come from a position of strength where you can offer help that the loved one is open to receiving.

Benefits of Knowing What to Expect

As you become more adept at practicing empathy, you know more about what reactions to expect from your loved ones before you even begin a conversation. You begin to get a feel for what circumstances affect them most and how they are likely to react to them. This understanding can help you offer welcome assistance and provide you with many benefits, too.

<u>Less Uncertainty</u>

Feeling uncertain about what will happen can keep you from offering needed help. Sometimes, when you feel this uncertainty, you might avoid engaging in a conversation about the problem. It holds you back from forming those long-lasting and healthy bonds that you want so much.

When you have a better idea of what to expect, you feel more confident in practicing empathy and offering help. You inspire the other person to trust you when you trust yourself more. The resulting interaction is likely to be more positive and productive.

Decreased Anxiety

Fear of the unknown can come over you in waves of anxiety, especially if you are concerned that you might damage your most cherished relationships. And, if you are anxious about a conversation, your anxiety can be contagious. The other person can pick up on your negative emotions. The conversation in such a case is likely to be very unproductive and can actually cause a rift between the two of you. When you have a good idea of what to expect, you can feel calmer and readier to face even the most difficult situations.

Fewer Misunderstandings

When you do not know what to expect, you are more likely to offer advice or help that the other person resents. By preparing yourself for each empathetic exchange, you pave the way for a more peaceful and productive conversation. You know what questions to ask and what help to offer. You can prevent hurting the other person's feelings or making them feel that you haven't tried to understand.

How to Prepare for Engaging Empathetically

Before you approach your friend or family member with the idea of being empathetic to their situation, prepare for the conversation. You can never control every variable or know with complete certainty what the other person is going to do. But, you can eliminate some of the uncertainty and anxiety and prevent misunderstandings by preparing yourself beforehand.

Understand What the Other Will Need from You

As you think of the other person and imagine them in their situation, think about their needs. Consider this list of needs and think about whether the other person's situation is keeping them from being fulfilled: food, water, shelter, security, warmth, sleep, stability, security, safety, a sense of belonging, affection, independence, self-respect and respect from others, realization of hopes and dreams.

After you go through this list, you are likely to notice some needs the person is not being able to meet. Before you set out to meet these needs, though, talk to the other person and make sure you are right. In the meantime, you can have a head start in thinking of ways to meet the needs you recognize.

Also, ask yourself if you are the one the person would like to meet each need? Your friend or family member might have a need for love and affection, but the love they lack might not be yours. For example, they might instead need romantic love or parental love that is not in your power to give to them. However, in these cases, there might be something you can do, even if it is simply to offer comfort and support.

Prepare Yourself for Upcoming Events and Conversations

Look at your calendar. What events are coming up in the near future that might be difficult for your friend or family member? If you think you will have a chance to talk to them, how can you help them get through the event? What can you say or do to make things better for the other person?

For instance, imagine that your friend's daughter is getting married. Further imagine that the friend's ex-husband has hurt your friend deeply and is going to be at the wedding. Think about the wedding day and the parts of the event that will allow you a chance to connect with your friend. Perhaps you can ask her over for dinner one night just before the wedding and talk to her about how you can help. Maybe you would have opportunities to connect with her during the reception. You can make plans to be there for your friend, and be ready to offer that needed support.

Imagining the situation in an empathetic way helps you know what to expect and prepare for it. So, as you think of the upcoming event, imagine how this person will react to this situation. How are they likely to feel about it? In the example above, it might seem obvious that anyone would feel anger, resentment, hurt or bitterness. However, your friend might take it differently. After all, she is a unique person. So, imagine this particular friend in this particular situation to be truly empathetic.

Sometimes, the events you need to prepare for are important conversations you plan to have with loved ones. You might need to discuss important topics like vacation plans, plans to move to a new residence or state, job decisions or parenting problems. By practicing empathetic imagining before the conversation, you can know what to expect and be prepared for it.

Know When to Bring Up Difficult Subjects

When you have a problem with a friend or family member, you can use empathy to help you resolve the conflict. You can have the best opportunity for a meaningful discussion if you time the conversation just right. Think about what time will offer the greatest possibility for a calm and productive conversation. Do you need to wait until your friend deals with another issue in their life? Would it be better to have the conversation immediately to avoid future problems? Imagining the friend's current situation empathetically can help you answer these questions so you know what to expect.

Be Ready to Respond Appropriately

By taking an empathetic view of your friend or family member's situation, you can prepare some possible responses to needs they might express. This allows you to escape that uncomfortable uncertainty and anxiety as well as avoid misunderstandings. Simply put yourself in their shoes and think of how they would like to be treated and what would be most helpful for them to hear. This is how knowing what to expect can increase the effectiveness of being empathetic and give you the power to make positive changes in your life and the lives of those you care about every day.

Yet you need to remember to stay flexible when you actually have the conversation. It is impossible for you to know or feel everything exactly as your loved one does. You can have a fairly good understanding of the situation, but the differences between you prevent empathy from being absolutely perfect. So, be ready for surprises as you proceed with the interaction to resolve your loved one's needs or any problems between the two of you.

Chapter 8: Connect with the Larger World

As you get better acquainted with your close circle and improve your most intimate relationships, you can also benefit from changing your perspective on the larger world. Not only will your view of other people become more accurate, but also you can find ways to help those in need and promote the social changes you would like to see in the world.

Does this sound rather ambitious to you? At first blush, it might seem like an impossible task. And certainly, you can't fix everything that is wrong in the world. However, what you can do is make a positive difference in whatever ways you choose. You can do it by empathizing with others outside your closest circle. As you do, you can inspire those you care about to make positive changes in the world as well.

See Other People More Accurately

How do you see others outside your close circle of friends and relatives? Are they somehow "different" from you? Of course they are different. First of all, they are unique individuals. Each of them has something valuable to give to their friends, family members and others around them. Each of them has strengths, weaknesses and issues to deal with just as you and those closest to you do.

Along with the personal differences, there are also cultural differences to be aware of as you think empathetically about others. Even those you know best may come from different cultures and backgrounds. Because you were not raised in the same type of social environment as they were, you can only understand them by learning about their culture and using empathy to imagine their lives more accurately.

Outside your closest circle are friends and family members you have yet to meet. There are also many other people you will never get the chance to know personally. At the same time, you can have an impact on their lives through charitable giving. You can volunteer your time to help those who have problems that you, your friends and your family members will never experience.

What does this have to do with practicing empathy to improve close, personal relationships? It does so by giving you the opportunity to unite your closest circle in accomplishing something meaningful in the larger world. As you and those closest to you give or volunteer side by side, you develop more positive relationships with them and galvanize them to work towards sharing your good fortune with others outside your circle. And that is one of the most amazing powers of empathizing with others.

Know the Best Ways to Help Others

Sending a check or clicking a button on a charity's website might seem like the easiest and surest way to help others. However, this form of giving does not bring people together. In addition, without doing research on the charity, you don't even know how much of the money will be used to help others or how they will be helped.

Even when you see what a charity is doing, you don't know if they are taking the most positive steps to help others if you do not make the effort to empathize with those who will be helped. Having empathy for those outside your close personal friends and family can be a difficult task. You know less about them and might not have a chance to engage in conversation with them.

However, when you find out as much as possible about them, you can put yourself in their shoes and encourage other family members to empathize as well. Those of you who stand together to help others in need can get to know each other better and appreciate the personal qualities you all bring to the larger world.

Promote Positive Social Change

Just as you want to help those closest to you, you can also help those less fortunate. You can practice empathy for people in other social statuses and work with your closest friends and family members to create positive changes in the social structure. You can work together to spread the word about a new program that is available to help people in poverty. You and your loved ones can band together to help those who have little power to improve their situations on their own.

So, what do you do if your friends and family do not share your vision? Keep empathizing with each of them on both major issues and small ones. Show you care about them first. Then, live your commitment to effecting the social changes you want to see. You will become a role model for the attitudes and behaviors that are most helpful in meeting your goals. At the same instant that you connect with those you hold most dear, you can connect with those outside your circle, and indeed with the larger world.

Conclusion

Now that you have received an introduction on how to practice empathy, go back and do the exercises if you have not already done them. Look at the examples once more and think about similar situations in your own life. You are well on your way to becoming a more empathetic, understanding person. And, you are closer to resolving conflicts and disagreements within your close circle of friends and family.

The next step is to go out and make your first attempts at imagining your loved ones' perspectives. Remember to consider their individuality and their unique situations as you picture what life is like for them. Think of what they need and how they would like to be treated. Use this empathetic understanding to prepare yourself for events and conversations that you need to have with each person in your closest circle.

Don't stop at imagining, either. Take those first steps on the road to becoming a more empathetic friend, spouse and family member. Show your loved ones that you understand their situation and recognize their need. Follow through with appropriate actions to improve both your life and the lives of those most important to you.

As you become skilled at expressing empathy for your closest friends and family, you are going to change all your lives for the better. Move forward now to provide the emotional and physical support your friends and family members need. Promote the changes you wish to see in your closest circle. If you do it empathetically, your world is about to become more peaceful and positive with each passing day. So, put aside your former role as a helpless bystander and engage your friends and family member in the meaningful interactions that can change your relationships completely. Create the reality you wish to live in now and every day into the future through positivity, caring and empathy.

Thank you for reading this book. We hope you found this information helpful and actionable.

Please write a review for this book and check out our other books on Amazon.

For more resources on relationships and to get in contact with us, please visit us on the web at http://www.relationshipup.com.

Printed in Great Britain
by Amazon.co.uk, Ltd.,
Marston Gate.